TRUTH IS—
WHY *Lie* NOW

Inspirational Rhyming Poems

LORRAINE SAAVEDRA

ISBN 978-1-63903-090-3 (paperback)
ISBN 978-1-63903-091-0 (digital)

Christian Faith Publishing, Inc.
832 Park Avenue
Meadville, PA 16335
www.christianfaithpublishing.com

All bible verses come from biblegateway.com and are (NIV) New International Version.

Printed in the United States of America

Contents

Forgiveness..7
The Shiny Tree..9
Never the Same 11
He Understands 13
He Has a Reason 15
Guardian Angel...17
God's Presence...19
The Only Way 21
God's Glory..23
Angel by My Side...25
Blessed by Faith...27
Never Ending Prayers 29
"He Is Risen"..31
Repentance...33
Light in Darkness..35
We Will Hug Again..37
A Simple Hello...39
Letting God Lead 41
Forgiving Others 43
The Will to Pray...45
This Little Cross..47
Taking a Chance..49
In Their Eyes..51
I Am Enough 53
Shining Beautifully......................................55
Six Hands to Hold 57
In His Hands 59
Time to Reflect 61
Blessed by Grace...63
God Has a Plan 65

Never Far Away 67
One More Mile 69
God's Intentions 71
I Am Never Last 73
Finding Courage 75
A New Day 77
We'll Be Okay 79
I Do Forgive 81
Because We Forgive 83
I Choose to Pray 85

But if you do not forgive others their sins,
your Father will not forgive your sins.

—Matthew 6:15

Forgiveness

If I take it slow
I know that I will grow;
I have so much to forgive
if I want to live.

Though the lesson isn't clear
I cannot leave it here;
I may not understand
but it is still His plan.

So I will beg and plead
that by mercy He will lead;
and as He shines His light
I know I'll do what's right.

7

The Shiny Tree

There was once a little Christmas tree,
that told a story of you and me;
the little tree shined so bright,
even though it had no lights.

When you put it in its place,
I saw the smile upon your face;
and I knew right from the very start,
just how much it filled your heart.

Then one day, you sent a photo shot,
and you had placed it in a pot;
I remember being so surprised,
that the tree was still alive.

I prayed the tree would never die,
because of what it signified;
I wonder where it is today,
now that our friendship has gone astray.

*In the beginning was the Word, and the Word
was with God, and the Word was God.*

—John 1:1

Never the Same

"Hallowed be Your name"
Your love is not a game;
if I live Your Word,
I will never be the same.

Though the evil one will try,
Your love, I won't deny;
because You live and died,
so that I may soar and fly.

*Even though I walk through the darkest
valley, I will fear no evil, for you are with me;
your rod and your staff, they comfort me.*

—Psalm 23:4

He Understands

I fear the thoughts that are in my head,
that come from the evil one;
that if I base my deliverance on them,
I am as good as done.

So I will plead God's daily bread,
and pray I am enough;
and then I'll hope He understands,
that things in life are tough.

By His mercy and His grace,
I might just see eternity;
for if I choose to live in Him,
then He will live in me.

*Carry each other's burdens, and in this
way you will fulfill the law of Christ.*

—Galatians 6:2

He Has a Reason

I hold a pain inside,
that I cannot define;
because I will not share,
I lost a friend who cares.

It tears my friend apart,
and breaks her loving heart;
but I cannot explain,
why I'm walking in the rain.

I'll ask the One who knows,
to mend my aching soul;
I know He has a reason,
and He will guide me in this season.

Blessed are those who mourn, for
they will be comforted.

—Matthew 5:4

Guardian Angel

When You called her home
my heart was all in pieces;
but as I woke each morning
I knew that it was Jesus.

On that very day
You showered me with love;
then my mother spoke to me
from heaven up above.

I felt her very presence
and I kissed her on the cheek;
and then a calm surrounded me
and I could barely speak.

The days that passed grew brighter
as I could clearly see;
I had a guardian angel
watching over me.

The Lord *is close to the brokenhearted and*
saves those who are crushed in spirit.

—Psalm 34:18

God's Presence

The timing of what is at hand,
I may not ever understand;
I live a life of joy and peace,
but on this day, it's filled with grief.

As I approach my latter years,
I find it hard to hold back tears;
because by faith, it's clear to see,
that You are always here with me.

I'm blessed to know that when I pray,
the pain I feel all goes away;
the very instant that I kneel,
Your love and peace are what I feel.

Hope deferred makes the heart sick, but
a longing fulfilled is a tree of life.

—Proverbs 13:12

The Only Way

My intentions were so pure,
but for a time, I wasn't sure;
with all the shame and pain,
I thought I'd never walk again.

My life was such a mess,
I had no choice, I guess;
I sought Your Holy Name,
You didn't hesitate—You came.

I grow a little more each day,
because there is no other Way;
though I may never understand,
I leave it in Your hand.

And the God of all grace, who called you to his eternal glory in Christ, after you have suffered a little while, will himself restore you and make you strong, firm and steadfast.

—1 Peter 5:10

God's Glory

I find comfort in my morning routine,
when God's glory surrounds me in my suffering.

As I praise His mercy and His grace,
His blinding light shines upon my face.

I know my pain is near its end,
and that my heart will heal again.

I thank Him that I grew to know,
the peace and love He always shows.

He gives me strength that I may be,
a light like Him for all to see.

Angel by My Side

I have a loving brother
who grew up by my side;
that if it wasn't for him,
I may not have survived.

The day our father passed
I wanted just to hide;
never mind the sadness,
and all the times I cried.

But now that I am older
my heart is filled with pride;
I have an angel in heaven,
and one here at my side.

I just want him to know
that I'm grateful and I'm glad;
for all the love he shares,
that I know he got from *Dad*.

Heal me, LORD, *and I will be healed; save me and I will be saved, for you are the one I praise.*

—Jeremiah 17:14

Blessed by Faith

We've faced a dreadful year
filled with anxiety and fear;
we've even lost acquaintances
and others we hold dear.

The devil wants to divide
but our God is so alive!
The pain that we've endured
only He himself can cure.

He calls us to believe
if we are to receive;
so I will not disparage
His promise or His message.

For I myself have grown
with all that He has shown;
yes, we have paid a cost
but the evil one has lost.

Though we have felt the pain
our blessing is our faith;
no, the virus wasn't fair
but God was always there.

*Greater love has no one than this: to lay
down one's life for one's friends.*

—John 15:13

Never Ending Prayers

Have you ever been confused
on if you're sad or mad,
because you suddenly lost
the best friend you ever had?

It's only now and then
that you meet that special friend,
and you want to be there by her side
but she has so much to hide.

She thought she wasn't enough
so I showered her with love,
and then the friendship ended
because she got offended.

Though months and years may pass
and oh, so very fast,
a day will never end
without praying for my friend.

So as I prayed today
I heard my Father say,
"My child, you are good,
you did the best you could."

When God raised up his servant, he sent him first to you to bless you by turning each of you from your wicked ways.

—Acts 3:26

"He Is Risen"

"He is Risen" on this day,
so that I may live in faith;
I am grateful because I see,
that He died for you and me.

Though I know I am not worthy,
of how He chose to love me;
the anguish that He faced,
says I am blessed by grace.

"Lord, because You died and live,
I know that You forgive;
and it's clear what I must do,
to please and honor You."

Godly sorrow brings repentance that
leads to salvation and leaves no regret,
but worldly sorrow brings death.

—2 Corinthians 7:10

Repentance

Until this very day
I still beat myself up,
because I lost my patience
with someone that I love.

Before You called her home
I wanted to confess,
that since the day her health went
my life was such a mess.

But now she's past the gate
and I hope it's not too late,
I no longer can pretend
if I want my heart to mend.

I have such deep regret
for the words that I had spoken,
"Please know they were not personal
and they left me sad and broken."

So as I kneel, I pray
Your mercy leads the way,
to forgiveness from our mothers
for me and many others.

My faith and hope have healed me
and I know I'm not alone,
I can't wait to embrace her
on the day You call me home.

Everyone who does evil hates the light,
and will not come into the light for fear
that their deeds will be exposed.

—John 3:20

Light in Darkness

As morning turns to night
and darkness steals my light;
I reach out for His hand
and pray He understands.

I tell Him I've made messes
and ask if He'll send lessons;
and then I hear Him say
that I am healed by grace.

I fall down on my knees
and thank the Lord above;
that He has blessed my life
with peace and hope and love.

Now as I close my eyes
everything shines bright;
for even in the darkness
He is my Guiding Light.

Let us hold unswervingly to the hope we profess, for he who promised is faithful.

—Hebrews 10:23

We Will Hug Again

I would run a million miles
to see your beautiful smile.
I would walk through snow and rain
to hug you once again.

I would take you by the hand
and say, "I understand."
I wish that I had known
that you were sad and broken.

Though you took your precious life
I know you're still alive;
for the God who's well and living
is understanding and forgiving.

Today I pictured your smile
as I sat for just a while;
and then I knelt to pray
and I thanked Him for His grace.

God hears me when I sigh
and He heals me when I cry;
He says He knows my pain
and that we will hug again.

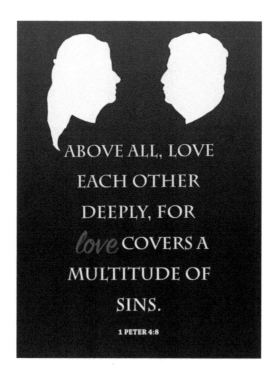

ABOVE ALL, LOVE EACH OTHER DEEPLY, FOR *love* COVERS A MULTITUDE OF SINS.

1 PETER 4:8

A Simple Hello

As we passed, we both said "Hello,"
but I was rushing to be on my way;
I was happy that he didn't let me go,
and content with what he had to say.

We'd made plans for dinner that night,
though my intentions were never to show;
as the time passed, it didn't seem right,
so I said, "What the heck, I'll just go."

Every night before bed I had prayed,
to have someone to love in my life;
it was the greatest decision I'd made,
before long we were husband and wife.

You blessed us with two loving children,
and we are grateful for the path You prepared;
we thank You for all that You've given,
and for the memories and love that we've shared.

I the Lord *search the heart and examine the mind, to reward each person according to their conduct, according to what their deeds deserve.*

—Jeremiah 17:10

Letting God Lead

"Blessed with determination" is what I was once told,
but I had never heard it, until I'd grown old.

That's a phrase that seems to fit me to a tee,
because never giving up,
is one of my strongest qualities.

It's important to share the core values that we have,
but if we've forgotten where we came from,
I don't think that we can.

Doing with the purest of intentions
is what I have sought,
because it is the way I had always been taught.

Acting out of love should be our
purpose and our goal,
so that our determination isn't
mistaken for wanting to control.

I, at times in my life, have been a bit forward,
and as a result, I have hurt people with my words.

Today I am determined to let God lead,
for only He can give us everything we need.

I apologize to those whom I have offended,
with the forgiveness of God,
my heart has been mended.

You, Lord, *are forgiving and good,*
abounding in love to all who call to you.

—Psalm 86:5

Forgiving Others

Relationships can end
with family and with friends;
though we may grow apart,
they never leave our hearts.

We argue and we fight
from morning until night;
then it hurts us to the touch,
because we said so much.

"Lord please lead us to forgiveness,
and heal the pain within us;
we trust You because You've shown,
that we can't do this on our own."

May the God of hope fill you with all joy and
peace as you trust in him, so that you may overflow
with hope by the power of the Holy Spirit.

—Romans 15:13

The Will to Pray

We have all been through so much,
so we just lie here in the dark;
it's difficult for us to discuss,
all the pain that fills our hearts.

We sigh with every breath,
and cry with each new day;
we've all been faced with death,
and don't even know what to say.

I think what hurts the most,
is that we claim to be okay;
but some of us aren't even close,
and we have lost the will to pray.

God knows when we are broken,
and He never leaves our side;
before words are even spoken,
He, too, has already cried.

He promises comfort and strength,
and that He will shine His light;
He heals when we pray in faith,
be it morning, noon, or night.

This Little Cross

I made this little cross to see,
if God would really comfort me;
because I walk most every day,
it's here that I would stop to pray.

I walk quite fast and very tall,
but on this day, I felt so small;
so I chose to drive a couple miles,
in hopes that we would reconcile.

Sadly the words my friend would say,
meant that I was turned away;
and when my friend did not repent,
I cried, "God, comfort wasn't sent!"

He said, "I know your concern was deep,
and this is why you often weep;
it's clear your efforts were sincere,
but first forgive, then leave it here."

I said, "Because You truly care,
my faith grows stronger with every prayer;
and while I'll admit that I still grieve,
this cross I made says, I believe!"

*If either of them falls down, one can help
the other up. But pity anyone who falls
and has no one to help them up.*

—Ecclesiastes 4:10

Taking a Chance

Do you ever wonder where you would be
if you hadn't taken a chance;
it's like being in the middle of the dance floor
and choosing not to dance.

I believe it's the same with the friendships
that we choose throughout our lives;
many will bring us that happiness
that will keep our souls alive.

But there will also be those others
with which the friendship will not last;
and whether we believe it or not
even they will leave an impact.

Now I am older and wiser
but I will never regret my past;
it seems the relationships I learned most from
were the ones that didn't last.

There were friends that broke my heart
and I wish that I had known;
but if I had not let them in
I never would have grown.

So I'll continue to make new friends
even though I am taking a chance;
and when given the opportunity
"I will always choose to dance."

*Humble yourselves, therefore, under God's mighty
hand, that he may lift you up in due time.
Cast all your anxiety on him because he cares for you.*

—1 Peter 5:6–7

In Their Eyes

As I journey through this life
as a mother and a wife;
I regret my past mistakes
so much, my heart it aches.

But if I let them get me down
my smile, it turns into a frown;
and then I miss the times I shined
in the eyes of these precious men of mine.

Before I know it, God is near
and He explains it all so clear;
because you love so very dear
they are grateful that you're here.

Instantly, I'm in a place
that brings a smile back to my face.

*I praise you because I am fearfully
and wonderfully made; your works are
wonderful, I know that full well.*

—Psalm 139:14

I Am Enough

Today I woke up with the sun,
and though my day had just begun;
I already had so much to say,
so I got down on my knees to pray.

There are days I wonder if I can,
and then You reach out for my hand;
but lately, life has been so tough,
it's left me wondering, "Am I enough?"

I've asked many women in my past;
"Why is it we put ourselves last?"
"No, you all go ahead of me"
is what we tell our family.

We give them all a great big kiss,
and convince ourselves, "We've got this!"
We're quick to do and love to give,
but sometimes we forget to live.

Now all our children have moved away,
and things seem different as we pray;
though it all happened very fast,
we sit and wonder why we're last.

Again I seek the Lord above,
and He reminds me I am loved;
He says He knows life can be rough,
and in His eyes, "I am enough."

I'm sure not all have felt the same,
but I am grateful that you came;
I hope that we can all agree,
we're blessed to have our family.

Shining Beautifully

She is beautiful and shines like the sun;
but today, she just feels out of place;
it seems her problems have just begun;
you could tell by the look on her face.

She had loved him since who knows when;
and was grateful every day for the bond;
but today, she just couldn't forget;
what she'd seen at the edge of the pond.

They'd been married for many years;
and had even been blessed with kids;
but today, the rejection drew tears,
because she couldn't forgive what he did.

She spoke to the Lord of the shame;
and the memories that roamed in her head;
she was honored each time that He came;
as she cried every night in her bed.

There are days when she grows and forgives;
and on others, she just wants to run;
but with every new day that she lives;
she shines beautifully again like the sun.

Six Hands to Hold

Once upon a time,
when I was only nine;
I wanted someone to explain,
why I was sad and felt such pain.

Was it because I had been bad,
that God had come to take my dad?
Why would He come from up above,
to take the man I dearly loved?

He was the only dad I had,
so I could never understand;
would God just send another man,
to come and take me by the hand?

For many years I failed to see,
that God was always there for me;
but now I know He, too, was sad,
that I had lost my precious dad.

Today I know God had a plan,
on whom He'd send to take my hand;
no wonder my heart is filled with joy,
He sent my husband and my boys.

If we take the time, we'll find,
the Lord above is loving and kind;
for the part of the story that's still untold,
is that now I have six hands to hold.

Do not conform to the pattern of this world, but
be transformed by the renewing of your mind.
Then you will be able to test and approve what
God's will is—his good, pleasing and perfect will.

—Romans 12:2

In His Hands

Today was better than the last,
in my search to find the real me;
I've survived many issues in my past,
so I just don't see how this could be.

I'm angry because I can't find peace,
on this path I'm faced with every day;
I'm tired of coming to my knees,
and still not knowing for what to pray.

I have my health and family too,
so I know that I am truly blessed;
but someone tell me what you do,
when on certain days you're still a mess.

It's true that we're supposed to hurt,
when someone passes unexpectedly;
but never when we've said kind words,
and loved so unconditionally.

Until I know the real reason,
I will fight my insecurities;
I can't believe I'm in this season,
with all of my responsibilities.

I've always heard God has a plan,
so I will trust Him and believe;
"Lord, I will leave this in Your hands,
but please, don't ask me not to grieve."

Let us then approach God's throne of grace with confidence, so that we may receive mercy and find grace to help us in our time of need.

—Hebrews 4:16

Time to Reflect

Oh, the knowledge we could all collect,
if we would take time to reflect;
I'm grateful I took that step back,
to find the faith I'd always lacked.

The perseverance in itself,
was way up high upon a shelf;
me always wanting to control,
had finally come to take its toll.

The reason I could not receive,
was that I struggled to believe;
but today, I can proudly say,
"Jesus Christ, You are the Way!"

The advice that I would humbly give,
is please, don't wait so long to live;
the only way to joy and peace,
is simply choosing to believe.

Friends, I'm not perfect in any way,
it's why I take the time to pray;
with everything that we have faced,
we're all in need of mercy and grace.

In their hearts humans plan their course,
but the LORD *establishes their steps.*

—Proverbs 16:9

Blessed by Grace

I am in a place,
where I am blessed by grace;
He who holds the stars,
heals my many scars.

And though I sometimes fall,
I know He hears my call;
and when I'm most distraught,
is when I will be caught.

It's when I'm on my knees,
that I feel His love and peace;
I find He's always close,
when I need Him the most.

"For I know the plans I have for
you," declares the LORD,
"plans to prosper you and not to harm you,
plans to give you hope and a future."

—Jeremiah 29:11

God Has a Plan

I never could quite understand,
why God would wait so patiently;
but now I know He has a plan,
and that He loves me unconditionally.

I regret that I was filled with pride,
for it got the very best of me;
back then, I had so much to hide,
that I didn't want the world to see.

I wish I'd listened long ago,
it wasn't that I hadn't heard;
I'd say, "I got this on my own,"
and refuse to listen to His Word.

It's clear that God is always here,
and we'll find Him if we do our part;
but He will never interfere,
if we choose to keep Him from our heart.

He promises "hope and a future" too,
but I know He'll give us even more;
so let us do what we must do,
to ensure His blessings are secure.

Trust in the LORD *with all your heart and lean not on your own understanding; in all your ways submit to him, and he will make your paths straight.*

—Proverbs 3:5–6

Never Far Away

A part of me trusts God's timing,
but the other part wants to control;
right now, everything is falling to pieces,
and I am desperate to make it whole.

You promised to never leave me,
but today You seem far away;
"Wait—give me a couple of minutes,
I believe I've forgotten to pray."

The evil one hears me praying,
so he's grumbling, but he's waiting;
he knows perseverance is difficult,
so he's sitting and anticipating.

He attempts to disrupt my plea,
and I despise his very presence;
but he knows if I lose my faith,
his timing is of essence.

God, You have never left my side,
so I will listen to Your voice;
I am determined to let You lead,
and I am glad I made that choice.

One More Mile

I wonder if I walked a while,
if I could ever find my smile?
I wake up and begin to clean,
and say, "I'm proud of my routine."

But there are times, I will confess,
that I would leave it all a mess;
so I could find the part of me,
that I had always hoped to be.

I work out nearly every day,
and all throughout the day I pray;
but somewhere I have lost my peace,
and all because I choose to please.

I convince them all that I'm okay,
because it's what I always say;
but way down deep within my heart,
I fear I'll never find that part.

No, I am not ashamed to say,
I did not make the bed today;
instead, I walked another mile,
and yes, I did, I found my smile.

*and if it does evil in my sight and does
not obey me, then I will reconsider the
good I had intended to do for it.*

—Jeremiah 18:10

God's Intentions

I see You in the night,
You are my guiding light;
a protector and a friend,
until the very end.

But I know that I must fear,
if I want to have You near;
and when I don't obey,
is when You're far away.

I've read it, and I've heard,
it's all there in Your Word;
if I choose to leave Your side,
it's best to run and hide.

I have fought the good fight, I have finished the race, I have kept the faith.

—2 Timothy 4:7

I Am Never Last

It seems the minute I close my eyes,
a million things run through my mind;
if you could only see the pace,
you'd think for sure I'd won the race.

When I was young, I had such fun,
because I'd use my legs to run;
back then my mind was always clear,
my legs were fast, and I had no fear.

But as I grow older reality sets in,
and all the challenges of life begin;
suddenly, my legs stop in their tracks,
and my mind's the only thing running fast.

While in my mind I sometimes fear,
I'm blessed to know the Lord is near;
yes, my legs are slower than in the past,
but in the eyes of God, "I am never last."

Get rid of bitterness, rage and anger, brawling and slander, along with every form of malice. Be kind and compassionate to one another, forgiving each other, just as in Christ God forgave you.

—Ephesians 4:31–32

Finding Courage

You can smile and you can laugh
but it is evidently clear
that from the pain of your past
you should no longer run;
yes, you can ignore it or even wait another year,
but the words to that song...they must be sung.

When you carry that weight and pain from your past
of how others have hurt you many times before,
it can get heavier and heavier exceedingly fast,
and you won't be content in this life anymore.

I know the things they did cut like a knife
and the words they used were painfully blunt;
but if you're ever going to live a peaceful life,
you must find the courage it takes to confront.

Can you imagine the healing your decision will bring
when you find it in your heart to grow and forgive?
You will finally be blessed with a new song to sing,
of the beautiful life you are destined to live.

I can do all this through him who gives me strength.

—Philippians 4:13

A New Day

How do we know when it's time to stop
those anxiety-filled compulsions that we adopt?
We refuse to admit because we're filled with pride,
that our obsessions are beginning
to consume us inside.

Now all that we've accomplished
throughout the years
is quickly diminishing and we are filled with tears;
but still, we convince ourselves
our problems aren't bad
when compared to the issues
that other people have.

Loved ones are concerned,
so we choose to stay away
because we don't want to hear
what they have to say.

Just how much longer can we continue to deny
that our addictions are beginning
to destroy our lives?

I know in our minds we're convinced we are tough,
but we have to understand when enough is enough.

So never give up and continue to pray,
because God is our strength, and it is a new day!

We remember before our God and Father
your work produced by faith, your labor
prompted by love, and your endurance
inspired by hope in our Lord Jesus Christ.

—1 Thessalonians 1:3

We'll Be Okay

Did you toss and turn again last night,
and did you cry out to Lord above?
With the crazy things that went through your mind,
did you forget that you are dearly loved?

When we worry about what others say,
their words can make us insecure;
but if we'll wake up and begin to pray,
we'll feel God's peace and love for sure.

Like you, I wish that I could see,
God's mighty plan for me today;
but if we will trust Him and believe,
with faith and hope, we'll be okay.

I Do Forgive

While I don't understand, why our friendship ended,
I can honestly say, my heart has finally mended.

Another thing I'll humbly say,
is that you made a huge mistake that day!
I don't know what went through your mind,
but a friend like me, you'll never find.

No, I'm not perfect in any way,
but I do have another thing to say;
all I did came from the heart,
and I sincerely believe I did my part.

The last thing I have left to say,
is that ending a friendship that way is not okay;
and for as long as you or I shall live,
"I must move on, but I do forgive."

And when you stand praying, if you hold anything
against anyone, forgive them, so that your
Father in heaven may forgive you your sins.

—Mark 11:25

Because We Forgive

The enemy loves to divide
when we are filled with pride;
so many relationships ended
because we got offended.

We choose to lose our friends
when we cannot make amends;
how can we stand and face
the One who saves by grace.

If we truly want to live;
we must learn to forgive.

*Now may the Lord of peace himself
give you peace at all times and in every
way. The Lord be with all of you.*

—2 Thessalonians 3:16

I Choose to Pray

I think it's time, before we leave
to stand and fight for what we believe;
just who we are, we'll never know
until we choose to take control.

In this world, we're doing fine
but the godly us, we'll never find;
until we take time to reveal
exactly how we really feel.

So as for me, I choose to pray,
regardless of what others say;
I know that God has paid a cost,
and if not for Him, I would be lost.

About the Author

Lorraine Saavedra was born and raised in Albuquerque's far north valley. She is the youngest of nine children (mostly boys) in a home abundant with faith and love. With the loss of her father at the early age of nine, she was determined to grow quickly and take responsibility for the health and well-being of her mother. At age twenty-six, she was blessed to meet and soon marry her husband of over twenty-six years and begin her own life. She and her husband raised (you guessed it) two boys. Her faith, life experiences, and continued determination have guided her in writing some of the deepest poetry imaginable to inspire and comfort others in this journey of life on earth. Her poetry could not have come at a better time, as we struggle to find our way during one of the most devastating global pandemics ever. Lorraine and her husband remained in Albuquerque, New Mexico.

CPSIA information can be obtained
at www.ICGtesting.com
Printed in the USA
BVHW062154220222
629765BV00023B/1016